Elizabeth Rapp

What the trees are telling me

To my dear friend Mary

with much love

Elisabeth.

Ash Wednesday 2016.

What the trees are telling me

Published by Poetry Space Ltd. 2015

© Poems Elizabeth Rapp

© Front cover image Fiona Watson

This edition first published in Great Britain in 2015

by Poetry Space Ltd.

Poetry Space Ltd. Company No. 7144469 All rights reserved.

Reg.office. 21 Davis Close, Barrs Court, Bristol, BS30 7BU

Printed and bound in Great Britain

by

Whitehall Printing Ltd, Bristol

ISBN: 978-1-909404-24-3

www.poetryspace.co.uk

In memory of

Tony Corner

mathematician and beloved husband

Elizabeth Rapp was brought up in rural Worcestershire which gave her a lasting love of the natural world and concern for ecology and animal welfare issues. She now lives in south Somerset where she is a tutor in Creative Writing and lectures on literary subjects at Dilington House Adult Education Centre. She also leads writing groups in the area and gives one to one sessions and poetry readings. Her poetry has been widely published in national magazines and five poems have won prizes in national poetry competitions.

Following two pamphlets her first full collection was published by David Perman at The Rockingham Press in 2000 and was launched at Dartington Festival and the Poetry Café in London.

She is a lay minister in the Church of England and has worked in Exeter Prison, with the homeless in Oxford and at Helen House, Oxford, the first children's hospice in the world.

She is a graduate teacher and has worked in both state schools and in the independent sector and with children with behavioural difficulties in residential communities.

Acknowledgements and thanks:-

To David Perman of The Rockingham Press for permission to print from **Dancing on Bones**: *Pharoah's Tomb, A Ring of Stones* and *Eating Pearls.*

My gratitude to David Cundy for his skill and patience in typing my collection and to Wendy for her support.

To Sue Sims for publishing my new collection and to Penelope Shuttle, Danielle Hope, Anne Stewart and Dr. R.V. Bailey for reading the manuscript, also for their helpful comments.

Second Light Network directed by Dilys Wood is a continuous source of stimulation, inspiration and support.

My thanks to members of Roadside Writers and Westport Poets for their encouragement and companionship as poets.

Finally to Fiona Watson for agreeing the use of her lovely painting *Songs Unsung* as a front cover image.

Contents

Persimmon Tree

PICKING ELDERFLOWERS AT MIDNIGHT

for Judy and Alastair

Dew numbs my bare feet as I stretch up
to pick elderblossom shining against
a blue-black dome speckled with stars.

Humpbacked sheep stir restlessly
as a badger snuffles in a nearby ditch,
a screech owl rips through the wood.

I'm gathering flowers in the Glebe Field
as I've done for twenty years –
like women from this cottage over centuries.

I share their gentle mystery
as I stoop for well water, cut lemons
which sting every nick in my skin.

I, too, create a miracle, transforming
insect-laden petals into nectar
cool and pure as moonlight.

mystery - Old English for skill in a craft

BREATH OF LOVE

these roses breathe out gentleness
as walls gather perfume into themselves
like a lovely secret

but do they miss the sun's bright energy
which unfurls their petals at dawn
peers into the golden calyx?

do they long for the wind's touch
blowing to and fro on pliant, slender stems
brushing my stone walls?

perhaps they desire the moon's cool glance
shiver at the owl's silent shadow
the fox's stealthy tread

but here they are, captured in a vase
colour of the sea wave's underbelly
as it falls on the shore

roses brush against frail Canterbury bells
sweet flutes of honeysuckle
clumps of Queen Anne's lace

exhale beauty, soft as an eider feather
delicate as a mulberry moth's silk thread
the bright beauty of a woman in love

HIBISCUS

You laid your glory at my feet
      falling from your bush –
a gorgeous cup of darkest red
      so soft, so fresh, so lush.

Your heart of deepest, fragrant fire
      soft as the bee's soft fur
frail as gossamer, transparent lace
      floats in living water now.

CHALICE

You are the cup
into which we pour
our turbulent pain.

By Love's mysterious alchemy
those bitter dark waters
become blood-red wine.

CHRYSALIS

For Brendan Kennelly

Here's my gift: a new heart, a sturdy heart,
its four chambers swept and garnished
with white and purple iris
heaped in silver lustre jugs
under windows opening onto hills
and a clear river white with sails;
all ready for me as I reach you
at last, after a long journey
through rough hill-country,
as I trudge in with muddy boots
and a rucksack filled
with dried apricots and rye bread,
brandy and home-made sloe gin;
a well-thumbed map which smells of garlic,
a compass set true north
and, hidden in one canvas corner,
the swelling chrysalis of an Emperor butterfly.

FEARLESS FRAN
for Wendy and David

She rows her way along the landing
in her fragile canoe, keeping a sharp eye
open for crocodiles and poisonous snakes,

listening to the raucous screams of monkeys,
glimpsing the scarlet flash of feathers
as exotic birds skim through the forest overhead.

She rows on bravely (renowned for her courage)
follows a bend in the river when suddenly
at the edge of a vast waterfall

her canoe capsizes, she is flung pell-mell,
helter-skelter into the hurly-burly
of a raging torrent, tossed like a stick

to and fro, upside down, until she comes to rest
on the silver sand of a tropical island.
She bumps down each stair on her bottom

then shuffles along the hallway to the kitchen.
Ahead she glimpses a village with mud huts,
a native woman stirring a huge cooking-pot.

"So this is the dreaded cannibal tribe ...
I'm sure they'll eat me for supper" Fran gasps
but her invincible courage never fails,

so she walks forward to meet her fate
straight into their kitchen where
her mother gives her a hug, kisses her.

"So there you are! Supper time. Tell me
what you've been doing – you've been so quiet"
Fran was tucking into her beans on toast.

"Nothing much" she mumbles, returns
to being just ordinary again.

AUBADE FOR A BLACKBIRD

My bright and beautiful blackbird
from the thick of the cherry tree
your song dissolves the dark,

pours music into the air –
light dancing, glancing on water.
Your eyes' gold ring weds you to sky.

One wing drifts in the breeze,
the other lies pinioned on tarmac:
I lift, cradle your cooling body,

stroke the crushed skull, mangled breast,
those fragile legs which hopped across the lawn,
gleaming feathers, clenched retracted claws.

Your lyric beak half opens
its aubade dies in your throat.

MOTHERING SUNDAY

Panic swirls round the room
as I clamber unsteadily from stool to ledge
to rescue you.

Time and again you flutter from my hands,
bang against the glass, bruising wings
neck, claws and beak.

But suddenly, you lie quiescent,
cradled in my hands,
neat head between my thumbs.

Your frantic heartbeat
pulses though my flesh
as I carry you to the open door,

sense the thrust and lift of life.
I uncup my hands and watch as you
speed into your primal element –

        freedom

REVELATION
after Deszi Kosztolanyi

Perhaps I understand what the trees are telling me,
signalling with their yellow fingers
from the intolerable shadow of no

while I sit on this terrace,
eating breakfast warmed by an autumn sun.
At my side, a glass tray incised with intertwining lines.

I look at the deep emerald bowl
fragrant with pear. Grapes I picked
at dawn shine with inner light.

A drop of dew sidles down a peach,
pauses, falls, scatters into a thousand fragments
on the cusp of yes and no.

WHISPER

In memoriam Bernard Lovell at Jodrell Bank

A clatter of schoolgirl sandals
clumps up metal stairs
into the dome in a field

on the Cheshire plain
into total darkness where
not a chink nor a mote

not a beam nor sliver
of light finds rest here.
Time holds its breath

as we stand motionless.
Silence deep and complete
fills us to the brim of thought.

Then comes a whisper, a hiss
passing through aeons, millennia,
light years, with a message

of creation over thirteen billion years ago.

PHARAOH'S TOMB

in memoriam John Rapp

Will there be time
to leave the shrouded house,
cross the darkening stream,
to where my father crouches,
mending a stone wall?

He wears shoes with broken toes
(kept for messy, outdoor jobs)
rumpled jeans tethered
with blue binder twine.

I pass him the trowel, watch,
as he dabs mortar on stone
as delicately as a woman
dabs varnish on her nails.

He weighs, balances, cuts
the facets with a neat clunk
of the hammer, then slides
the last stone into place:
like the final block
which sealed the Pharaoh's tomb
until profane hands looted its treasure.

Will there be time
to gather up the tools,
brush the path clear
of sand and chippings,
amble back to the house,

laughing about the Morris 8
he built from scratch
with those same scholar's hands
which inscribed Greek
with scrupulous love?

FAMILY ALBUM

Aged thirty, she nestles against
a friend's shadowed shoulder.

My mother dressed in blue lace,
precarious kid leather shoes.

A silk bandeau gathers her harvest hair,
her eyes signal a faint alarm.

I wonder why she cowers so
from the probing lens?

Perhaps she fears that winters to come
will fret away fragile lace, flesh and reason.

TIME

Time is an old man
I carry on my shoulders.

Sometimes he jumps down
and runs across the fields

trampling down ripe wheat
stumbling over broken stones

following the silver deer at dawn
until he turns to clamber

onto my back – he is
my indestructible burden.

GRANDMA

Dad would tell me how she sat slimwaisted,
upright, playing her Eberhardt piano
in the evening – Chopin nocturnes, Viennese waltzes,

Moody and Sankey hymns for chapel.
Sometimes, in a low, clear voice
she would sing folksongs of forsaken love.

> *Firelight played on her loose auburn hair*
> *as small birds flew from the keys*
> *to weave nests of song around the house.*

Those strong white hands crocheted lace,
embroidered linen, tooled leather blotters,
covers for rare editions.

She clothed my dolls with scraps of silk and lace,
an astrakhan coat and hat for Mary Parker,
dared to wear trousers when cycling round town.

She taught at the local orphanage,
nurtured lost and frightened refugees,
loved and rescued homeless cats,

but in later life she grew strange and wild,
took to roaming streets in her nightdress
until guided home by a kindly policeman.

Mistrusting everyone, fearing plots and poison,
she attacked a child with a carving knife,
starved her family of cats.

Her swift grace became unsteady amblings,
muttering, she wandered from room to room
until one night she had a fatal fall.

Firelight played on her loose auburn hair
as small birds flew from the keys
to weave nests of song around the house.

A RING OF STONES

The healing place is a ring of stones
where my father lifts an axe to fell
an ash tree hung with golden fruit.
He has the strength of a pedigree bull.

My mother dances a matador's dance,
teases the bull with a bloodstained cloth.
She hides her face behind a veil
woven from dust and linnet's feathers.

My brother drifts in a purple hammock,
swings between two stones: plays chess
against himself but always loses.
We do not speak. Nobody speaks.

I am a young goat chained to a pole
bleating with terror, with hunger, with thirst.
My father stops chopping the tree. My mother
stops dancing. My brother picks up a knife.

GREY SWEATER

in memoriam Helen Richards

From all the elegant clothes you left behind
I chose just one: a sweater soft as goose down,
as easy on my back
as sunshine on fells
cropped by sheep.
The colour of clouds sweeping over hills,
it smelt of clover and trodden grass,
of sharp north winds, harbingers of snow.

That was twenty years ago:
today I pull it from the drawer,
slip it over my head,
hear children's laughter
as I flick chalk from the sleeve.

THIRTEEN WAYS OF LOOKING AT A LAMB

(after Wallace Stevens)

Irrepressible ping-pong ball
bouncing on nature's trampoline

Glutton's delight flavoured
with mint sauce
a savoury Sunday roast

You gambol on Easter cards
among improbable daffodils

A stiff cold carcass
hung on a butcher's hook
waits for knife and cleaver

Shivering shorn lamb
we stole your fur coat

A cottonwool body
upheld by matchsticks –
a child's first icon

Stranded on a rocky ledge
you bleat for rescue in vain

In a desert feast
your eyes a tasty morsel
offered to a royal guest

Bottle-fed lamb grown big and strong
butts me as I open the gate

Emblem of salvation
innocent sacrifice
reigns victorious

Shy young lovers gaze at each other
with sheep's eyes

This gentle creature faces
the heraldic lion. One day
they will lie down together.

On damp church walls sheep
and goats pass to heaven or hell.

HUNKIN MILLENNIUM WOOD

for Christine and Jonathan

Drawn by the love which moves the sun, we gather
in this wood to celebrate a vision of hope:
the old, the young, the lame, the strong, pass through
the granite gateway forged by fire.

We are all children of the four elements –
fire, water, air and earth. We stand encircled
by the River Culm, rich land beneath our feet
with fire at its core, the cloud-tumbled sky above.

The river gleams with light from stars and moon,
as a sleek-furred otter slips through its amber depths
but we must leave womb's watery cradle
for the welcome of the stone baptismal font.

The Word was fire in the primal blast, creating time
from eternity, spinning all creation into life.
Gigantic flames at our planet's heart
and the flame of love at Whitsuntide – a gift for all.

The soil's strong back carries our roads, factories
and homes with patient endurance, but here
no plough will till this field. Wild flowers nod
among rough tussocks where grasshoppers sing.

Our children dug holes and planted saplings
with young and eager hands. They also dig our future,
grow tall, bear fruit, will shout and laugh around the wood:
their children, too will climb the granite gateway into life.

Air is angel's food, the breath of life unseen.
It bears a heron's croaking flight across the brindled sky,
carries children's laughter round a war-torn world but listen – !
the wingbeats of a thousand silver doves of peace pass overhead.

SCAPEGOAT

Following the lane's curve,
first the stink of randy goat
overpowers the drift of bluebells
and meadowsweet.

Then I see him hobbling
in tight circles,
his cloven hooves tangled
by a tethered rope.

He bleats softly, bends his head,
inviting touch. Moving close,
I gently stroke his beard,
feel his misshapen horns

lying flat against his skull,
trace his sharp-edged bones,
his hollow belly.
From his dusty coat

hairs blow away in the wind
like shriven sins.
Deep in his pale eyes I see
vast deserts

where his forebears wandered alone,
cast out to die of hunger and thirst.

MY CAT JENNY

is showing off
as I push open my garden gate.

She leaps up the fig tree to sway
unsteadily on the topmost branch,

watches me in triumph,
demands fulsome praise. Which I give.

Honour satisfied, she scrambles down
to the path, sits

all wildness vanished, demurely washes
her thick black fur gleaming in sunlight.

This is her new kingdom after rescue
starving and deaf from a wintry car park.

HEDGEHOGS
A true story

Shocked by the bloody corpse on the lane,
hearing a piteous, tiny squeaking

from five orphaned hedgehogs,
each no larger than a mouse,

stumbling round their nest
blindly seeking warmth and milk,

we cradled them home in our pockets,
put them in a box by the Aga,

drip fed them every two hours
until I was sent to bed.

How I loved them: their blind eyes
and purplish bumps like goose pimples

sprouting on their soft white skin –
incipient spears.

Rushing downstairs next morning, at dawn,
I found the box empty.

What desolation! What passionate grief!
Then our cat, proud mother of four,

called to me from her basket:
there I saw, curled up together

hedgehogs and kittens kneading her milky belly,
eager tiny mouths, suckling life.

GULLS' FLIGHT

for Wayne

Mud and muscle struggle.
Bitter wind and a brightening sun
as I clump across clay soil towards
a tractor ploughing a stubborn field.

Sudden lightening in the sky
as a flock of white-breasted gulls
wheels, swirls silently among cirrus clouds,
drifts like first flakes of snow

onto the earth to peck and stab
for worms and larvae. Then, as if they heard
some command, they rise as one
into the air, play with thermals,

flutter down, folding themselves neatly,
paper sculptures sitting
like pristine mushrooms on the furrows.
Two buzzards menace overhead.

My every atom and molecule leap
with the song of the wind and sky,
a hundred white-breasted birds,
as they fly beyond my understanding.

LUNATIC LIGHT

I wake with a start of terror
to the interrogator's power –
I am a prisoner under arc lights.

Startled and uneasy, I grope my way
to the kitchen where every cup, saucepan,
piece of fruit is lit by white fire.

Through the velux window I watch her –
immaculate and cruel
in her unquenchable brilliance.

She is devouring the smudge of darkness.
Impossible to drift into sleep
so I pace the house, the garden, till dawn.

Trees and flowers glisten with a metallic sheen
their soft and subtle selves lost,
made garish by this megalomaniac moon.

SHADOWS

Waking in an icy cave
in the whimpering dark,
she stumbled to her mother's bed,
claiming sanctuary.

"Nightmares again?
Let's play at shadows ..."
Three-year-old eyes followed
crooked fingers and thumbs

waving deftly against the candle-flame.
A huge fox loomed on the ceiling,
chased a rabbit to the kill.
She watched it stagger, twitch and die.

A LITTLE NIGHT MUSIC

my house weaves music
round me while I sleep

stones sigh, stir and settle
old bones on the earth

the dry cough of floorboards
as weightless feet pass by

skinflakes of the dead
settle in my lungs

blot up the day's wet ink as a rose
taps a secret code on glass

but down the stairs, beyond the door
I hear the clack of the treadle

hiss of spit on iron
the soft swish of a fallen dress

clatter of clogs on the flags
dying sigh of ash on the hearth

BOLHAM WATER

alone with a cool wind
I walk along the rim of the world

beside a field of flax pellucid
as a pool of pure water

a skylark sings its way into a froth
of curdled white clouds

below, a farmhouse dwindles against the hill
as I walk along the rim of the world

alone. complete.

ARIADNE AUF NAXOS

A ghazal

Sobbing, she runs along the shore at Naxos,
hears the receding splash of his oars.

Seaweed withers on the sand and rocks at Naxos.
Her huge black dog guards the bronze palace doors.

She tears her silken robes from breast to thigh at Naxos.
Her servants gorge fine food from the palace store.

Her pet caged birds chirp sleepily at dawn in Naxos.
Hunters set out to kill a wild boar.

Now he has forgotten her lovely face at Naxos.
A rainbow spreads its beauty without flaw.

She is dying of grief in her palace at Naxos.
Her callous maids are breaking every law.

He is sailing stormy seas far away from Naxos.
An old witch prophesies war.

MYCENAE

Weary of war, bloody mud and lice,
young men who whimper "mother" in their sleep,
he crosses the Argolid plain,
scans the forgotten landscape
for familiar landmarks –
a hill fort, a shepherd's hut.

It's been ten years since he led
his army, marching with spears,
shields flashing in the rising sun.
How sure they had been
of the gods' protection,
his glory in single combat.

He remembers the voyage,
hungry slaves rowing the ships,
rain sodden tents under the city walls,
widows waiting through the long nights,
stench of putrefying wounds
but oh! the glory of Hector's death.

He rides under the Lion gate
into the courtyard of his palace,
where the Queen awaits him with her maids.
Her face is thinner, bone-sharp, offers
a voluptuous smile beneath cold eyes.
Her magnificent hair reminds him of his daughter, Iphigenia.

Her cry of welcome makes him uneasy,
is like his whore's love cry, so
he pushes her away as he dismounts,
tossing the reins to a household slave.
The ten years' campaign had blotted out
the splendour of his kingdom's palace.

Now the Queen bows before him, holding
a bolt of purple silk which shimmers in the sun.
Deftly she throws it down the marble steps,
a river of blood – begs him walk on it
before a ritual cleansing of the stain of war,
offering sacrifice for his safe return.

He fears the anger of the gods at this hubris,
demurs, hesitates. She begs, pleads,
flatters, cajoles. Pride and vanity win.
He slips off his sandals,
treads on the priceless dye, sacred to the gods,
steps towards his fate.

SNAIL'S PACE

You run, yelling blue murder,
sword slashing sunlight

round those impregnable walls
pursuing your quarry

until, exhausted, Hector sinks,
helpless before the final blow.

Dragged at your chariot wheels
he becomes a lump of bleeding meat.

I, too, who lie felled by your fatal weakness,
wonder who you really are?

Golden boy of a blind poet's spin –
warrior … icon … butcher … thug?

Who am I, with mortal ankles,
snapped tendon, hobbled and housebound?

Achilles and I share the same mystery
as the snail tucked inside his shell

invisible till he emerges on his one foot
slowly, slowly writing silver lines

across his kingdom
as I do on mine.

WIMPLED LADY

O wimpled lady, lying so still on your stone bed,
what are you dreaming of, seven centuries dead?

> I dream of my oxen, my sheep and my cows
> as I breathe in the motes of my derelict house.

O my lovely lady, before blood turned to stone,
did you hear the owls' cry, the eastern wind's moan,
the laughter of children, the shuffle of feet?

> No – the prayers of the priest make my own death com-
> plete.

O stone-still lady, did you run in the wind, tumble from trees,
teach the hornbook to children as they stood at your knees,
order your household with your jangling black keys,
make mead from the honey culled from your bees?

> My hands raised in prayer are now worn away,
> which once kneaded bread, dandled babies in play,
> spun fine woollen thread, shuttled the loom,
> polished our pewter, spring-cleaned each room.

O worn and ancient lady, I kneel by your shrine,
your body so slim, is now frozen in time,
can you hear my heart beat or see my eyes shine
as I touch your cold face, warm your hands in mine?

> Yes, I see, hear and feel through all these sad years,
> lost are my dreams, my love and my tears:
> I know at world's end, when we shall all die,
> I'll be just a whisper, a spun thread, a sigh.

IN THE TWINKLING OF AN EYE ...

Here they sit, old, grey, forgotten.
Their eyes gaze into the past,
their future proffers endless bowls of soup.

Tucked, like babies, into their high chairs,
with crocheted rugs, a zimmer frame
bounds their horizon.

But do they ever long, these old ones,
to leap from their orthopaedic seat,
fling themselves through the fireproof doors,

their bodies lithe and free from pain,
hair wild as they dance through the air,
with breath as sweet as an April dawn?

SHADES OF TIME

She hung the "closed" sign on the door,
left the darkened room with its clutter
of books and bottles, the spiral staircase
leading nowhere. The parrot in his cage
squawked in terror. The smell of rancid milk
and damp clung to her coat and hair.

Twisting the key in a double lock
she walked away into a new dimension,
a different time. The printed words slipped
and slid off the page till nothing was left
of her life and name: nothing but
a dark blank space in the street's façade.

TIME IS A RIVER WITHOUT BANKS
by Marc Chagall

His fish flies in a world
    of calm blue light
        with wings of fire
            glowing scales:

plays to a million stars
    swoops and glides
        through a twilight land
            with houses, fields

where naked lovers create
    their own harmony
        with the spheres,
            the newborn moon.

The yellow pendulum
    in the carved case
        suspends movement
            for all eternity to listen

intently to the music
    the river's course,
        the lover's breath.

THE MAGIC OF LIGHT

Monet fell in love with light,
captured its magic on stone and glass:
Rouen Cathedral in early morning sun
the sharp focus of noon
evenings' gentle shadows.
Then water and light:
water lilies' shimmering reflections
in his lake.

Also entranced by the play of light and shade,
I paint with words.
Woken by birdsong at dawn,
I am drawn into the element of silver mist
where nothing is solid – mere hints
of shed, hedge, trees and house.

Mist nibbles away at my skin and bones,
face, fingers and toes.
I drift to the quiet blur of the pond
where I slip into a lily's white heart.

THE EAR

Vincent paces the yellow floor
exuberant with Provençal sun.

He remembers Theo, bills,
his mistress, his quarrel with Gauguin.

Is sharply hungry for a meal,
aubergines and peaches. Muscatel.

As the church clock strikes eleven,
he listens for the thunder,

watches rooks fly in agitation
over stooks of corn.

He puts his razor to his ear.

THE ARCHITECT'S HANDS

See the clipped nails, moon-shaped cuticles
a touch of ink on the index pad
I never could scrub out.

Feel the brush between thumb and finger
conjuring shimmering beauty
from marble, gold and lapis lazuli.

The Empress' tomb – the Taj Mahal
reflected in wavering water,
created from desperate grief.

The Emperor's reward …
elephants laden with jewels
poured like sunlight at my feet.

Then his festering fear
I might create another miracle
surpassing this.

So, today, came his dreaded command.
He allows me a few hours
to caress my wife, pick some lemons,

stroke my child's bright hair.
For the last time,
I shall peel a nectarine

before his swordsman comes
and lifts my hands
onto the royal block.

ARMISTICE DAY

Let's suppose
that all the men, women and children
who died, unripe in war,

gathered together on a mountain top
in, let's say, Tibet and opened wide,
wide as the sky their beseeching mouths –

what then?
What sound would they make –
would anyone listen?

Would the sound be the padding
of a wolf's claws across a dark forest floor
or waves in a fathomless cave

or the slow opening of a sunflower
to the sun, so that a bullfinch
might peck ripe seeds and live

or the soft rustling of a crocodile baby
held safe in his mother's mouth?

SANTA FE RAG

Bang bang, you're dead in Santa Fe
if you're a child and your ma's away
and your pa's a drunk, your sister's a slag,
so you sleep in a box and your blanket's a rag.

At morning light the street cleaner comes
with his big black brush and his hidden guns:
he's a sagging old man with a cringing dog
and he goes bang bang – then you're stiff as a log.

A man rolls by in a black limousine,
his cigars are the fattest you ever have seen
and his suit's handmade and his shirt is white
and he hates street children with all his might:

they mess up his city, they spoil his fun,
their eyes are so sad, he shoots with his gun
but people don't see or hear that bad noise
as the street cleaner sweeps away the dead boys

with his street cleaning trolley with wheels as bright
as a gold chocolate dollar traded at night
with crack in the sweetie to make you jump –
the street children stagger and fall with a thump.

 Bang bang, you're dead in Santa Fe
if you're a child and your ma's away
and your pa's a drunk and your sister's a slag,
so you sleep in a box and your blanket's a rag.

FIBONACCI POEM IN REVERSE

Look!

Water

summonsed from

trembling secret depths

it flows over stones, roots,

old bones, Ilium's treasure, thunderous power of waterfalls

slow, melting glaciers, creep of silt-heavy floods for farmers crouching in muddy fields

to plant seed for families dependent on this annual miracle while in the garden white

butterflies dance in the wind as

pollen-laden bees fumble for nectar, sway and flutter from lavender to hollyhock, dance and
meet in vibrant sunshine

like the ghosts of lost babies, as the sturdy yew trees wait patiently for consoling rain.

Consoling

rain!

sturdy yew

trees wait patiently –

rain flows over roots, stones,

Ilium's treasure, thunderous power of waterfalls, slow- melting glaciers,

creep of silt-heavy floods for farmers crouching in muddy fields to plant seed

while in this garden butterflies dance in the wind like the ghosts of lost babies, as the sturdy

yew trees wait

for rain summonsed from trembling secret depths, slow-melting glaciers flowing over stones,

roots, bones, Ilium's vast treasure

offering life from precious seed to family and cattle, while white butterflies dance in the wind.

ON LOOKING AT A PHOTO OF FIREFLIES

Splinters of moonlight shimmer in the air,
dart and dance among the trees turned blue
by night's dark art.

Such lights are the call to love –
a gentle lure to willing mates,
sexual signal, DNA's insistent pull.

Radiance suddenly vanishes until
brides-to-be accept this declaration
with a subdued glint, muted, shy.

Now I no longer stand in this wood
Nor savour the scent of trodden moss
Nor feel a soft summer wind on my cheek

but sit in spring sunlight in the home of friends,
instead recall the garden of an olive press in Corfu:
how, one evening a multitude of fireflies

flitted through the air, blazing tiny trails through darkness
which lit up spears of cypress, a water wheel,
distant glint of a pool. Cicadas chirruped

as we stood motionless, enchanted,
among myriad fireflies writing silver lines of love
on the dark page of night.

THE HAVEN OF THY RESURRECTION
Bairrie of Cork

Who is this heap of rags the wind blows through?

    I am this soldier, dauntless in battle.

Whose is this body, loitering under lamplight?

    I am this lily, her unpolluted flesh.

Who is this old woman, battered in her bed?

    I am this bride offering white roses.

Whose is this shadow, vaporised in concrete?

    I am this toddler dancing among leaves.

Whose flesh, bomb-strewn lies scattered on the earth?

    It is my flesh but risen from the grave.

Who is this baby radiant in a dark cave?

    I am this child, who bears the whole world's grief –
    the haven of thy resurrection.

ELIJAH

"a sound of sheer silence" 1 Kings 19 v.12

After defeat, flight and terror
the desolate prophet cowered
at the cave's mouth.

He watched as mountains split apart
rocks shattered rocks to splinters –
creation in turmoil.

Fire raged across the land
licked clean the forests of cedar,
turned earth to ashes.

> Then the gift of sheer silence
> fell on the waiting world.

I stand at my front door,
watch the winter sun
sink below the horizon.

I cannot hear even
the blink of an owl's eye
or the unfurling of an iris

> but only the crack of the primal egg
> God's indrawn breath of delight.

WHAT I WANT TO SAY …

can't be told. It lies buried
beneath an iron tongue –
a broken clapper in an ancient bell
inscribed with lost hieroglyphs.

It lies buried under skyscrapers
with the last Sioux whose shrine
is a theme park complete with
souvenirs of their lost tribe.

It is the silenced song
of a harpooned whale thrashing
his helpless body in the
roiling, bloodstained sea.

It is the muffled cry of men
deep in a northern seabed
shrouded in steel, dying slowly
of hunger thirst and cold.

It is the shudder of falling pillars
in burnt-out palaces of Troy,
gasping breath of men
who die in putrid trenches.

Oh! The impossibility of words.
But listen! The dry whisper
of a cast-off shroud explodes
through every atom in the universe.

AN AFTERNOON HAIKU
IN THE ALCAZAR GARDENS

toddler claps fat hands
in Queen Isabel's bedroom
ignores protocol

proud fantailed peacock
pecks fruitlessly at baked earth
bows down feathered crown

rill bisects courtyard
sun dances on still waters
listens to silence

marble colonnades
plastered walls and brilliant tiles
ripple in deep pools

tourists laugh gossip
unsure in deep labyrinth
escape with relief

garden of the poets
compels my full attention –
alas! just bare earth

two ducks are happy
in the splashing fountain head
preen bright green feathers

lovers sit entwined
hidden in a myrtle grove
startled by a dog

children laugh, race around
the Sultan's palace gardens –
do they sense his ghost?

sipping wine alone,
peacock struts past my table
why doesn't he bow?

EATING PEARLS

I shimmer and dart along terraces of water
which fall and rise with the restless salt tide.
I evade men's deadly nets.

Soft arms and hands have melted
into ribs, become bony fins.
Legs and feet have fused into my tail.

I swim through gaping eyes
of the silent shipwreck,
whose ghosts gently whisper my name,

Bubbles float from my mouth,
vowels on a heavy page of water.
I eat pearls prised from tight cradles.

I flick, twist and turn
my fish-body in my new element,
the swaying, dim and speckled sea.

CYCLE RIDE IN CORFU

You only noticed me when
I tipped you off your bike but

when you lift me in your hands,
warm me at your cheek

you cradle ten million years.
I began in a tumult of burning lava

spewed up through the earth's young crust,
flung into sea to be pummelled

by the surge and suck of tides,
picked up on the shore by patient hands –

women squatting by the Euphrates
where I pounded soiled cloth.

I am the fatal stone which felled the Philistine ox:
there I lay in the parched river bed

until you stumbled over me, took me home.
Today my beauty lies in silence, stillness

but if you smash me open
you will break my heart.

RAZOR'S EDGE

Sweating, bruised by rocks, I clamber
to the summit of Petra's holy mountain.
Breathless, I reach its small plateau
of sand, trodden earth, trinkets for sale.

A radiant Arab boy sits crosslegged
playing a pipe: music floats across
the ancient valley of pagan altars,
toppled pillars, carved palace façades.

He is playing at the very edge
of a three thousand foot drop
as an eagle wheels round and through
slow white clouds
                    vast   slow   white   clouds.

SAILING BY ....

12.30 a.m. A chilly sleepless night
when through the airwaves
"sailing by" and a bright boat
bobbing over sparkling waves
enters the darkness.

And I'm clutching the canvas sides
of a converted orange box,
trailing three-year-old fingers
through amber water, past rosebay willow herb.
My father pulls the boat along.

In daylight I steer my own boat,
stand at the prow of my frame,
leave the safe shore of my bed to push off
across the carpet, navigate narrow straits
between dresser and wardrobe.

I reach the clear blue passage where letters
are delivered, friends call in for a chat.
I gaze beyond the harbour wall
and see the ferryman wave from the river's edge.
So, grasping my two oboli, I sail slowly to meet him.

MAD TROMBONE

On a night when the wind
was breaking the neck of the woods,

when a parrot, a lizard and seven cats
slept hugger-mugger in a flower-pot,

when the test match score
made England blush bright red,

when I waited a second week
for your letter on the mat,

when my toes curled with longing
to dance with you all night,

when the television threw snow
all over Gardener's World

and my neighbour phoned to say
a mad Buddhist had burnt down

their museum of model aeroplanes,
when a blind bumble bee hit a daisy

WHAM-BAM and knocked itself out cold,
that very same day I decided

it was time to travel abroad.

So I picked up my Pianta di Venezia
where the Grand Canal meanders

like a mad trombone spawning young
all over the page, or like the twigs

and branches of a stricken tree,
or like the large intestine snaking

through the body of a replete man,
or like the blood vessels which burst

in your eye when you asked me to …

A JOURNEY BLINDFOLD

The gentle cropping of her breath
the band of bone around my ribs:
I am both ship and sea, rudder and sail,
air and glass, a wavering flame inside.

Single blue sail flaps on a green pond,
slices tight against the wind:
smack of water against the bow,
shock waves chill my hands.

I am giant to this Lilliput boat
shoved across a duck-congested pond.
I am four and a quarter,
tag along with my brother.

I am shingles and angles,
the hit of iron and the slap of weed.
Flame curves around glass and is safe
from the amber wind of the north.

A FLYTING
for the IT BUFF who erased all my poems

I wish you meltdown, IT buff –
it's time you knew I've had enough
of all your tricks and wasteful ways
erasing all the work of days –
poems, sonnets, epics all –
you pressed "delete"' but never called
to ask me if I would forestall
your wicked task
and so I ask
Apollo, god of sun and light
to use his power with all his might:
a little mouse soon you shall be –
but not the same as in IT –
you will be furry, soft and dumb
nibbling cheese with crust and crumb –
just anything your wife might bake.

You're doomed to run about your house
on tiny feet and sharpened teeth
until your wife wreaks her revenge
grabs your tail and then upends
you, soft and furry little mouse,
no more to scurry through her house,
little guessing you're her spouse.

So, IT buff, beware, beware –
 – treat my masterpiece with care!

ONLY ONE DAY REMAINS ...

From the shadows of the alley,
the dagger strikes

As the ice axe loosens,
an abyss swallows its prey

To the rattle of dice, the clink of glass
the unsinkable ship sinks

A child recites his seven times table
a woman mends her husband's shirt

as tectonic plates shift and grind,
an inferno lays waste to the earth

On that last day, how could they know
that only one day remained?

FIELD OF VISION
A glose for Antony Gormley

It is possible, I suppose, that sometime
      we will learn everything
there is to learn: what the world is, for example,
      and what it means.
                  (Mary Oliver)

What it means to be human, to feel our heart beat
      with a thousand longings
when our bones ache with desire
      our skulls fill with memories of loss and decay –
then it is possible, I suppose, that sometime
      we will learn everything?

What it is to be human, to enter an ancient house
      to search, like eager children
for treasure we believe is hidden in a foreign cave
      but which, too late, we find lies within us: -
what the world is, for example
      and what it means:

What it is to vault towards the highest bar
      but find our pole snaps beneath our weight,
to seek an Eldorado over the horizon
      but which, when found, is a barren wasteland?
So what is it to be human, to learn everything
      there is to learn?

Perhaps it is to stare at a thousand pair of eyes
      which gaze silently back at us – tiny figures
each one, clay of our earth, dust of our bones,
      searching for a poet's tongue
which will show us what the world is
      and what it means.

THRESHOLD

Disarmed, cross-legged, back
pressed against the stone wall
of my darkened cottage.

Starlight. A misty sickle moon,
mild summer's night,
a brooding silence

broken by a screech owl's cry
some small fragile creature
rustles among leaves.

I wait … and wait … when suddenly
I hear him scrunch along gravel,
grunt as he heaves himself into the porch.

Scrabble, snuffle as he scoops up peanuts
flips over the coir mat to gobble up the stash
of food I hide there each night. Our secret game.

Now I hold my breath: will he cross
the threshold of fear and danger to enter
a human house, encounter me?

Slowly, the white stripes of his mask
shine in the twilight, as he shuffles towards me
looking round curiously, without fear.

He peers at me, sniffs my feet and jeans,
places front paws on the wall, then drops down
on all fours, waddles across the carpet, unperturbed

explores the bottom stair, my empty fireplace,
the cat's litter tray, returns to my lap.
A hand's breadth away, I smell his bristly pelt,

watch his sharp teeth peaceably munch nuts
his scimitar claws an inch from my bare feet;
he looks up from time to time, gives little grunts

of pleasure, then replete, wanders off
to the door, stumpy tail brushing the floor.
I wait motionless and cramped.

Where is he? If I get up I may frighten him.
Or is he halfway up the field to his sett?
I unfold stiffly, lock the door ready for bed

Halfway up the stairs, I hear a familiar scuffle
ambling up the path – then a thump on the old oak door.
I pause … it comes again … and again: But

I leave it shut against his demand, beloved friend
longed-for visitor who trusted me so deeply:
was this a shameful betrayal or was it wisdom?

PERSIMMON TREE

CAMPING IN FIESOLE

We pitched our tent at the edge of the field,
         under a cypress tree overlooking the Umbrian plain
where the Arno slithers under toy bridges
         towards a city of statues, domes, palazzos,
drifting lovers and Guide Bleu tourists.

By day we peered at dim frescoed churches
         jumped across shadows of thirteen tall towers,
walked around Dante's simple house in exile
         its front door pierced by two holes for his cats.
We gazed in awe at Petrarch's dusty laurel wreath.

In the evening I crouched over the Gaz stove
         while you were reading The Divine Comedy.
I scrubbed burnt saucepans under starlight
         humming arias or singing the latest hits.
At night we lay apart. You snored.

A lifetime on, I stand where our tent stood.
         The cypress is felled. Needles, broken glass
lager cans lie scattered on the worn earth.
         The long dark years confront me
like a broken-backed bridge I cannot cross.

THE MAKER'S HOUSE

Outside, raw earth, broken bricks,
one struggling blade of wheat.

Inside, a white and spacious room
gracious as love.

In one corner a huddle of smooth stones
where brittle seaweed sharpens the air.

On the floor a child's sailing boat:
from its gashed prow pour priceless gems.

maker: Old English word for poet

GRIEF

is a fathomless salt lake
in a strange land

its waters dark and still
monsters lurk in its caves

birds of prey stalk along its shore
scavenging corpses

my bones are stone
about to break

MESSAGES

Summer is a-cumen in
lhude sing cuckoo
(medieval carol)

With hands smelling of onion,
gripping the kitchen knife,
impatiently she picks up the phone.

> from the garden
> lhude sings cuckoo
> three score years plus two

A thin trickle of words down the line
asks about an expensive hearing aid:
a drop of water from an empty cistern.

> from the garden
> lhude sing
> in a ring, a ring …

Words flutter like torn paper
driven by a cold wind:
her reply a heavy sack of stones.

> from the garden
> cuckoo, cuckoo
> death looks for you

She waits dumb and still,
hands in her lap by the phone:
she has become stone.

> but in the garden
> sumer is a-cumen in
> despite grief, despite sin

They tell her not to come today,
but visit the mortuary tomorrow.

       and in the garden
       silence, sorrow.

HARVEST TIME

You fell at harvest time,
when the lanes were thick with leaves
as if in Vallambrosa.

Oak trees throw down their tiny bullets,
which squirrels deftly hold as they
strip out their sweetness.

I pick plump, juicy blackberries
to make your favourite pie,
as if you were still here.

Broken by lightning, sunk in earth,
our apple tree has a dying crop
of mottled, wizened fruit.

Crab apples litter the earth, discarded coins.
Blackbirds gorge on elderberries,
everywhere a wild abundance

a ripple of bronze, scarlet, gold
a mad extravagance of seeds, leaves and berries
a flourish of dying splendour.

And everywhere you are not.

PARALLEL LINES

Lulled by the rocking rhythm of the train,
I watch gleaming tracks run towards infinity
but realise they never meet.

Travelling towards the horizon
searching for whatever lies beyond,
see it vanish into aether.

Stumbling across the Sinai desert,
dying of thirst, I saw a bright oasis,
found it was a mirage.

In a puddle, I see singing birds
in cloud-capped trees stretch to a boundless sky –
a footstep shatters all.

Memories are too shallow
for your reality, unreachable, untouchable now:
they vanish as I try to hold you fast.

PERSIMMON TREE
A Sestina

As I rummage through your boxes, I find your father's watch,
his army number ATP 143 engraved on its silver back.
Each night your stubby fingers wound its spring, placed it by your
bed.
You never knew your father in his witty, charming days,
before war's chaos destroyed his smiling calm.
Did he trap your sunlight, drag it underground?

Born in French Shanghai in a house with spacious grounds
you climbed an old persimmon tree, sat for hours to watch
the shingled roofs and palaces, the Bund's unspoilt calm
before Japan invaded: but its beauty never could come back.
Your father prospered in those halcyon, pre-war days,
so what terror made you weep when you were put to bed?

You soaked up language like bread in wine – chatting Mandarin in
bed –
you sang Russian folk songs as you played in the grounds.
Then Japan invaded China: in days
your home was looted, locked and lost. Your parents watched
each other slowly starve to death because they gave back
their food to save your life with sacrificial calm.

Then, peace declared, the world returned to a ghostly calm,
In an English small hotel you didn't even own a bed.
Then off to Cambridge with its glorious Backs,
punts on the Cam, old colleges in cloistered grounds.
When your father died, he left you his watch.
Then came the flowering of all your academic days.

Your passion for pure algebra filled your days
and nights as you searched for truth with profound calm,

80

I often saw you weep as you looked back
at those hungry, frightened years in camp and all the days
when as a child you should have found fresh ground
in Shanghai, nurtured in a place of loving calm.
Your wartime nightmares still haunted you in bed,
but through all these troubled times you still wore your father's
watch.

I kneel on the ground, wearing your father's watch,
weep by the rosemary bed, know you can't come back.
But through all the following months and years, the turbulent sea
grows still and calm.

WHITE STONE

Because it bears your name,
I crack open the white stone
on the sharp edge of my love,

to find bright jewels
scatter into my cupped hands.

WEARING YOUR ANORAK

I shrug it on, miles too big,
the sleeves flop over my hands,
its waist falls round my hips.

Walking here and there
sheltered from frost and rain,
the faint tang of your sweat,

a white hair on the sleeve
a gentle touch on my arm
become my flesh and blood.

INVISIBLE SUN

"Life is a pure flame and we live by an invisible sun"
Sir Thomas Browne

As I heave our suitcase from under the eaves,
brush off the dust of years, I see our initials
you painted so proudly, shine on the lid.

I test it in the passage, but one wheel is missing:
it falters, falls, the catch breaks open. Our dreams
and laughter fly out, pervade our home.

I hear the whistling wind of Wadi Rum,
the Berbers' black tent where we sit cross-legged
beside a brazier, dip our fingers into a communal stew.

Raw music as men whirl on bended knee, blur round and round
until they fall exhausted on the beaten earth. We stumble
from the tent across shifting sands under vast stars.

This suitcase comes with us to Fiesole where we eat
apricots warm from overhanging trees on the terrace,
gaze, enchanted, at the palazzos and domes of Florence below.

Green geckoes slither across the path as we wander
hand in hand past the Brownings' villa nearby,
listen to a stone fountain singing of mountain snow.

Then your sun's brightness becomes eclipsed by grief.
Nearly blind, you see only half my face: hallucinations are
the brain's atonement for your lost sight.

Your stubby fingers, once so quick and deft,
fumble over your computer and clavichord,
but tenderly stroke your beloved cat.

Today I watch by your bed as you lie wired to a monitor,
trace in your suffering face the young child who sat
in a persimmon tree in Shanghai, spitting pips on passers-by.

You were eight when the Japanese invaded China,
interned you all in a concentration camp
where you slowly starved until the Allies rescued you.

I hold in my hand a memento of this time, a penknife
you carved in hospital with the date of your liberation,
your parents' names: Lucy and Leonard Corner, August 17th 1945.

Now a lifetime on, in another hospital, I stroke your hands
and absent face, gently wrap you round and round
with silken threads of love.

Your first whispered words, after days of silence:
"You were calling, calling me, so I turned back …"
You survived another seven years.

Afterwards, all ceremonies over, I lift my wedding dress
from our suitcase. It still holds the scent of a June day:
cut grass, elder blossom, earth after rain.

Silk chiffon shimmers in autumn sunlight.
A row of silk buttons march up my back,
erect as guests waiting for the bridegroom.

The deepcut bodice, the flowing skirt,
gleam like a summer garden: - rose of early dawn,
blue of a thrush's egg, silver of birch bark.

I hold it against my ageing body, marvel at its fragile beauty,
stroke its softness, lay it to rest in my suitcase
folded like a shroud.

SEVILLE ORANGES

January the first.
Our garden huddles under frost –
white spears of grass stab the air.

As I open your last pot of marmalade,
I see you half blind, absorbed,
finding the exact angle of the knife

to sever rind, pith and flesh
then watch over the golden magma
as it broils and bubbles to setting point.

Such sharp fragrance sends me scrambling
up the Cretan mountainside
to St Nicolas' chapel, a thousand years old,

frescoes fading into dripping rock,
in a courtyard thick with trodden Sevilles.
We burst their bitter skins – then I hear

the sound of Ariadne weeping –
inconsolable on her god-forsaken island
devouring the horizon for her lover

who will never return.

GRIT

So often I see, just ahead of me
your slight form,

your head which enfolds
a brilliant brain

your half-blind eyes which search for solidity
in a world of strange shapes

mouth and tongue which lecture on abstruse theorems
flow with many languages

stubby fingers, one with a golden band
which only death would remove

hands which grope across your clavichord
but stroke our cat so tenderly

your feet with a broken toe
which travel the world

… and your worn-out heart which just stopped
suddenly, unexpectedly that night –

all these I hold in a fistful of grit,
let it trickle slowly through my hands.